ANIMAL COLORING BOOK

I0710758

This Book Belongs To

....

....

....

COLOR TEST PAGE

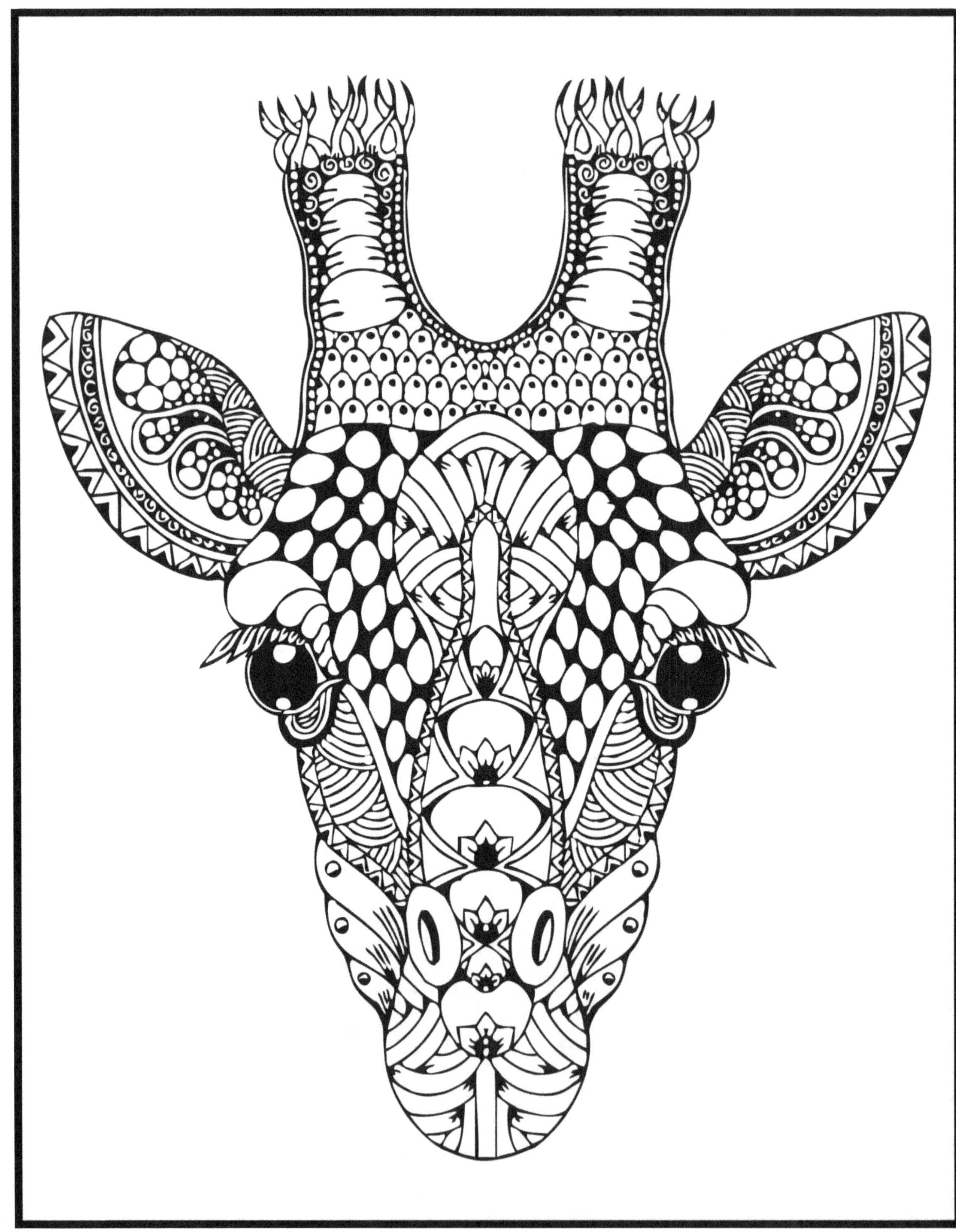

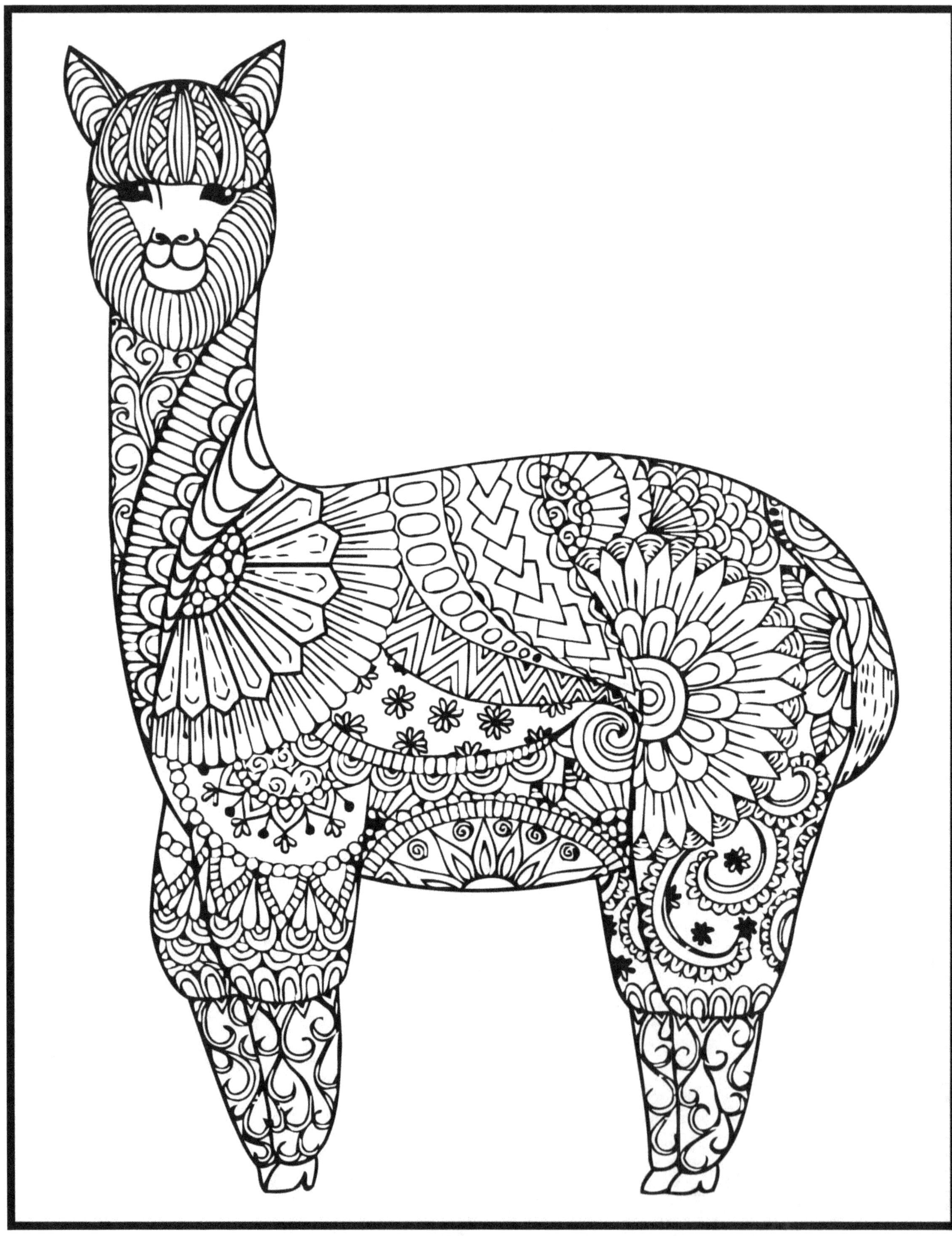

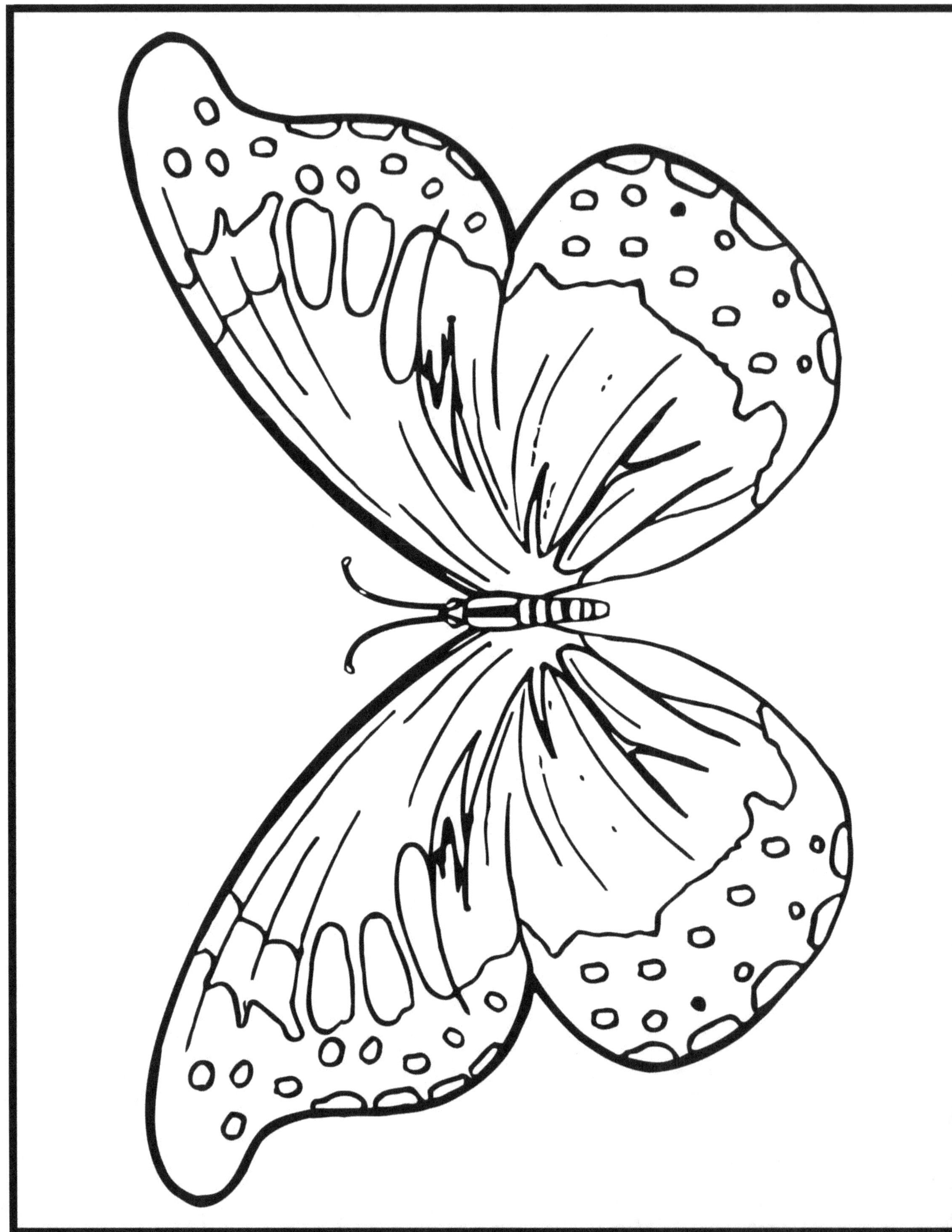

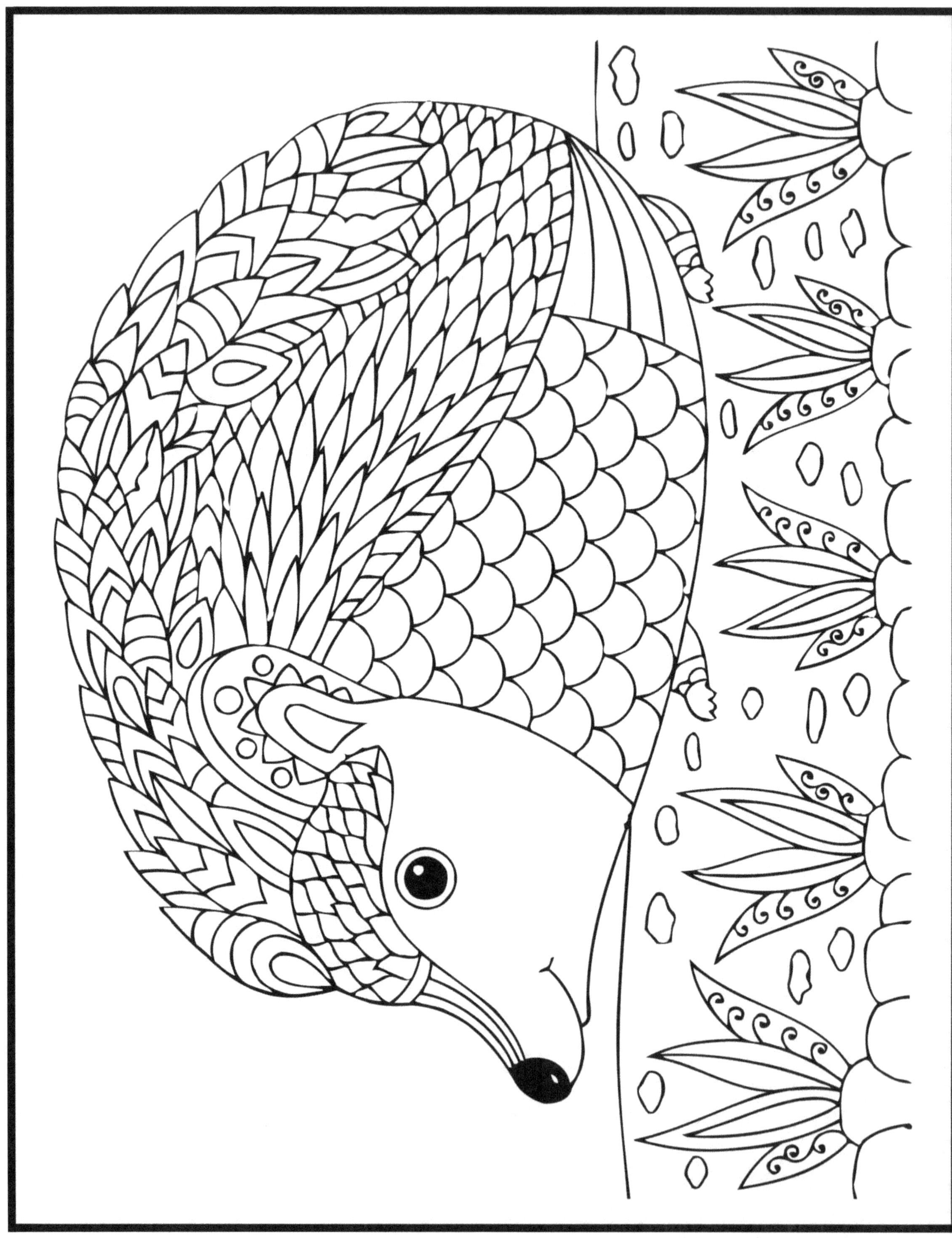

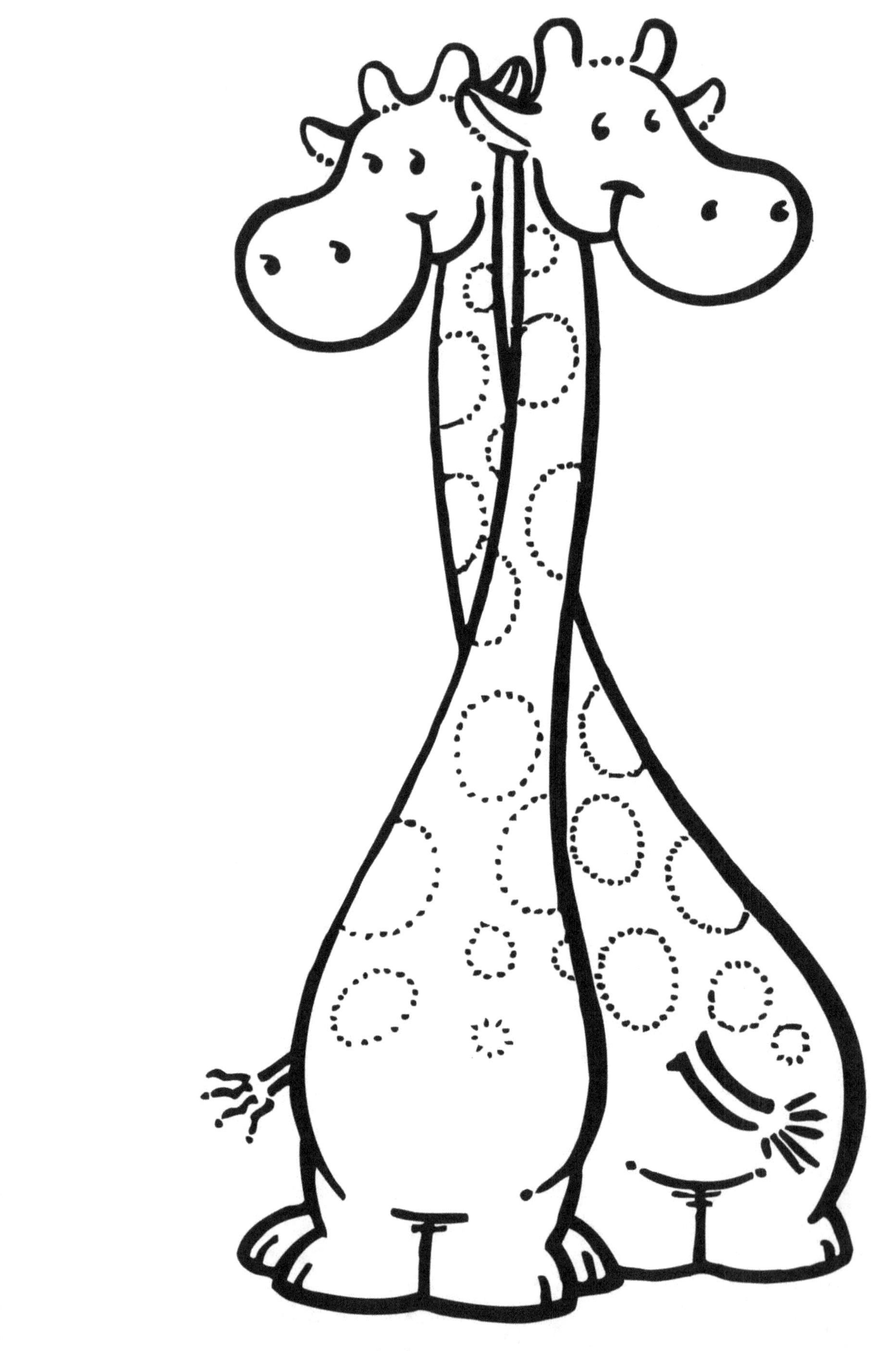

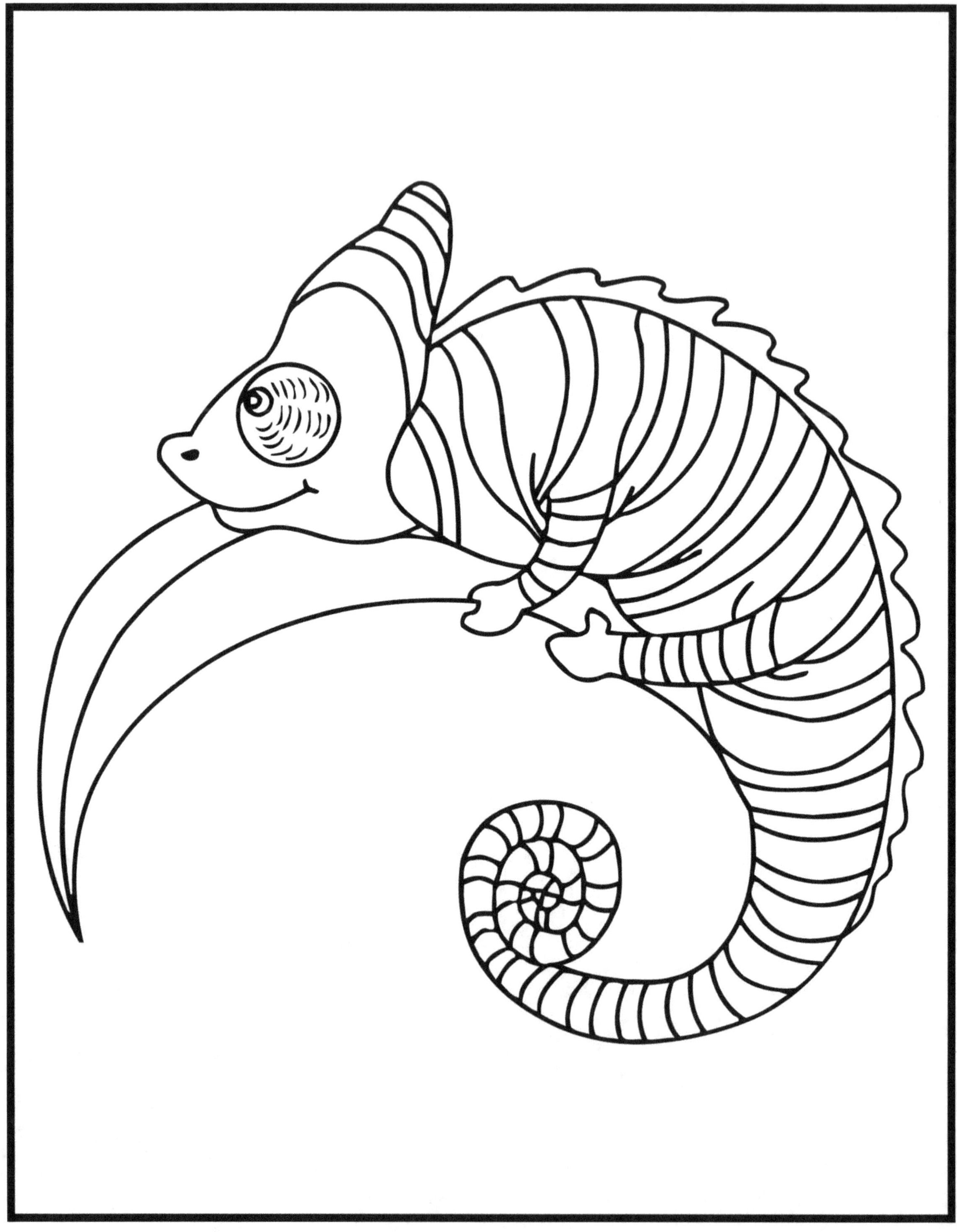

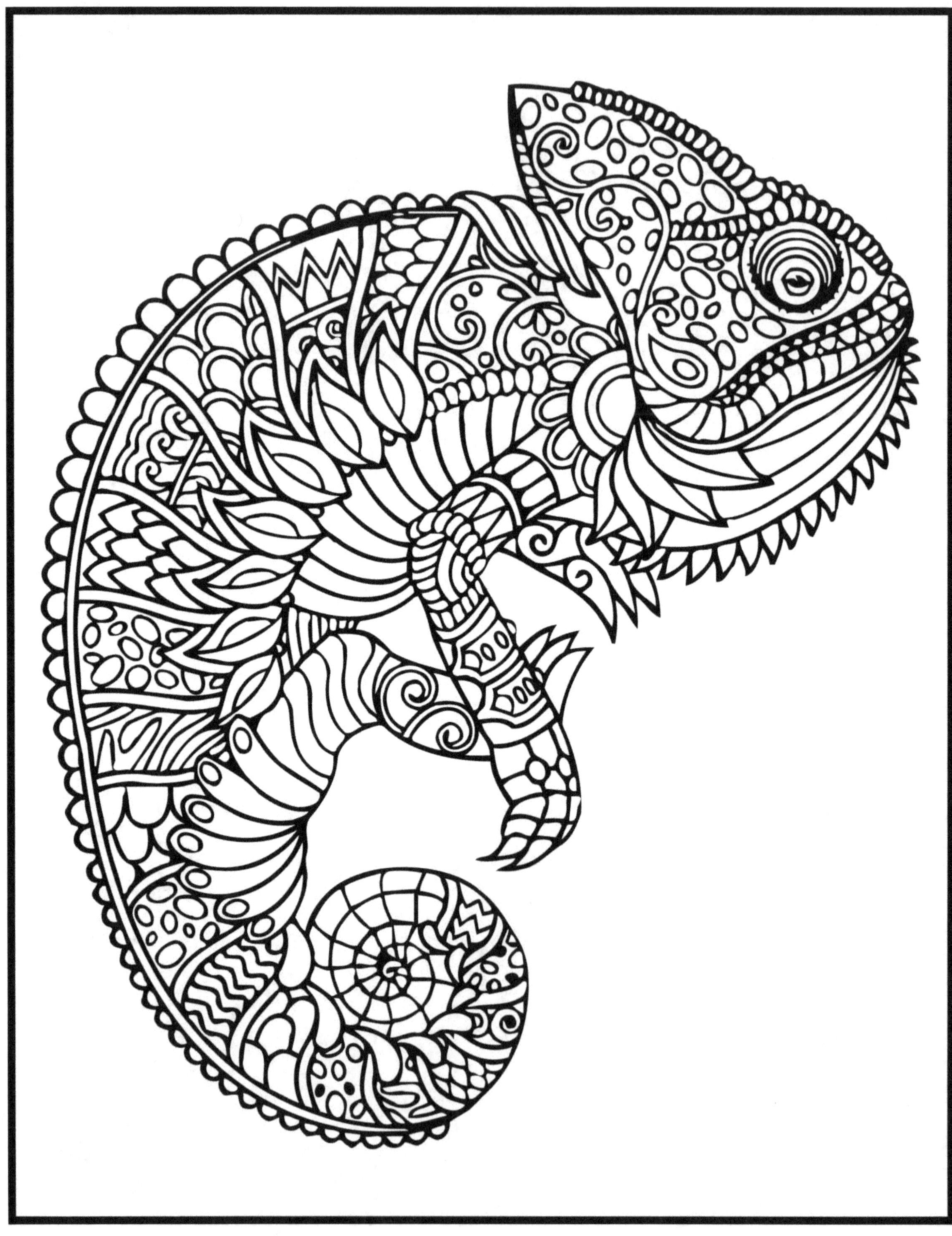

www.ingramcontent.com/pod-product-compliance
Lightning Source LLC
Chambersburg PA
CBHW081440250726
48662CB00009B/2882